BARYONYX

and Other Dinosaurs of the Isle of Wight Digs in England

by Dougal Dixon

illustrated by
Steve Weston and **James Field**

PICTURE WINDOW BOOKS
Minneapolis, Minnesota

Picture Window Books
151 Good Counsel Drive
P.O. Box 669
Mankato, MN 56002-0669
877-845-8392
www.picturewindowbooks.com

Printed in the United States of America.

 All books published by Picture Window Books
are manufactured with paper containing at
least 10 percent post-consumer waste.

Library of Congress Cataloging-in-Publication Data
Dixon, Dougal.
Baryonyx and other dinosaurs of the Isle of Wight
digs in England / by Dougal Dixon ; illustrated by
Steve Weston and James Field.
p. cm. — (Dinosaur find)
Includes index.
ISBN 978-1-4048-4719-4 (library binding)
1. Baryonyx—Juvenile literature. 2. Dinosaurs—
England—Wight, Isle of—Juvenile literature.
3. Paleontology—England—Wight, Isle of—Juvenile
literature. I. Weston, Steve, ill. II. Field,
James, 1959- ill. III. Title.
QE862.S3D5925 2009
567.909422'8—dc22   2008006344

Acknowledgments
This book was produced for Picture Window Books
by Bender Richardson White, U.K.

Illustrations by James Field (cover and pages 4–5, 7,
11, 15, 19) and Steve Weston (pages 9, 13, 17, 21).
Diagrams by Stefan Chabluk.

Photographs: iStockphoto pages 6 (Steven
Robertson), 8 (Valerie Crafter), 10 (Mike Rogal), 12
(Wolfgang Steiner), 14 (Liz Leyden), 16 (Axel Rieder),
18 (Abdolhamid Ebrahimi), 20 (Daniel Cardiff).

Consultant: John Stidworthy, Scientific Fellow of
the Zoological Society, London, and former
Lecturer in the Education Department, Natural
History Museum, London.

Types of dinosaurs
In this book, a red shape at the
top of a left-hand page shows
the animal was a meat-eater.
A green shape shows it was
a plant-eater.

Just how big—or small—
were they?
Dinosaurs were many different
sizes. We have compared their
size to one of the following:

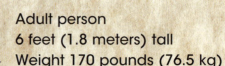

Chicken
2 feet (60 centimeters) tall
Weight 6 pounds (2.7 kilograms)

Adult person
6 feet (1.8 meters) tall
Weight 170 pounds (76.5 kg)

Elephant
10 feet (3 m) tall
Weight 12,000 pounds
(5,400 kg)

TABLE OF CONTENTS

WHAT'S INSIDE?

Dinosaurs! These dinosaurs lived on what is now the Isle of Wight, off the coast of southern England. Find out how they survived millions of years ago and what they have in common with today's animals.

LIFE ON THE ISLE OF WIGHT

Dinosaurs lived between 230 million and 65 million years ago. The world did not look the same then. Much of the land and many of the seas were not in the same places as they are now. The Isle of Wight, off the southern coast of England, was a region of swampy ground between upland areas.

A herd of *Iguanodon* crossed a swamp. A few small *Hypsilophodon* ran alongside them. A fierce *Baryonyx* watched them. But for now, the *Baryonyx* was busy catching fish in the shallow waters.

5

HYPSILOPHODON

Pronunciation:
HIP-see-LOH-foh-don

Hypsilophodon was a small, two-footed plant-eating dinosaur. It grazed the horsetail plants that grew at the side of the water. *Hypsilophodon's* legs were built for running. However, if the area suddenly flooded, the dinosaur would not be able to run away from the danger.

Swamp animals today

A modern crane nests in a swampy area near a river mouth, just as *Hypsilophodon* would have done long ago.

Size Comparison

A group of *Hypsilophodon* munched the tough stems of the horsetails that grew by the shallow water. They used their chisel-like teeth to chop up the food.

7

IGUANODON

Pronunciation:
ih-GWAN-o-dahn

Iguanodon was a big plant-eater. It ate the low-growing horsetail plants and the twigs and needles of conifer trees that grew in the swamps. Each of *Iguanodon*'s thumbs had a spike for tearing branches. Its little fingers also worked like thumbs.

Special hands today

The modern giant panda uses a pad on each of its paws to hold bamboo shoots. *Iguanodon* once used its thumbs in the same way.

Size Comparison

An *Iguanodon* stood up on its hind legs to reach into a tree and tear off twigs and needles to eat.

YAVERLANDIA

Pronunciation:
YAV-ur-LAN-dee-uh

Yaverlandia was a plant-eating dinosaur with a thick skull. The animal used its skull as a battering ram when defending itself against meat-eating dinosaurs. *Yaverlandia* also used its skull when fighting with other *Yaverlandia* to decide which individual would lead the herd.

Hard heads today

Modern deer push one another with their heads when they fight, just like *Yaverlandia* once did.

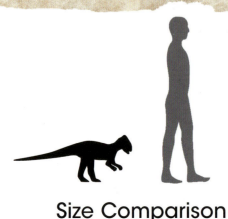

Size Comparison

There was a fight in the herd of *Yaverlandia*. Both of the big males wanted to lead the herd. The stronger one pushed the other away and became the leader.

POLACANTHUS

Pronunciation:
POH-luh-KAN-thus

A big armored dinosaur of the ancient swamps was *Polacanthus*. It had plates down the tail, a shield over its hips, and spikes on the shoulders. Meat-eating dinosaurs kept away from this tanklike animal.

Armored animals today

The modern white rhinoceros is protected by its thick skin, just as *Polacanthus* once was.

Size Comparison

A *Polacanthus* grazed peacefully in the horsetail beds. It ignored the meat-eating dinosaurs prowling around. *Polacanthus'* thick armor was too tough for the meat-eaters.

PELOROSAURUS

Pronunciation:
PEL-or-uh-SAW-rus

Pelorosaurus was one of the long-necked, plant-eating dinosaurs that lived in the horsetail swamps. It used a long neck to feed from the high branches of the few trees that grew in the area.

Migrating animals today

Modern zebras move from one feeding ground to another, just like *Pelorosaurus* once moved around in search of more food.

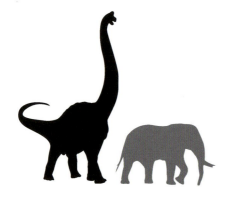

Size Comparison

A herd of *Pelorosaurus* had eaten all they could from the trees. They had to cross the swamp to find more food.

15

ARISTOSUCHUS

Pronunciation:
AH-ris-toe-SUE-chus

Small meat-eating dinosaurs ate small prey. *Aristosuchus* fed on the insects that were common in the area at that time. Bigger dinosaurs sometimes disturbed the insects. *Aristosuchus* would have caught the insects as they flew away.

Insect followers today

Today, birds eat insects just as *Aristosuchus* once did. When a plow disturbs the insects, the birds catch them.

Size Comparison

A herd of heavy *Pelorosaurus* churned up the mud, and insects flew out. Little *Aristosuchus* followed, feasting on the insects.

17

BARYONYX

Baryonyx was a big dinosaur with long, crocodile-like jaws and teeth. It had a big claw on each hand. *Baryonyx* was a fish-eating dinosaur. Scientists know this because they have found fossils of fish scales in its stomach.

Modern fish eaters

The modern heron stands in the water and catches fish with its long beak, just like *Baryonyx* once did with its long jaws.

Size Comparison

18

In total stillness, a big *Baryonyx* stood ankle-deep in the water. When a fish swam by, *Baryonyx* snapped it up using long jaws and sharp little teeth.

EOTYRANNUS

Pronunciation:
EE-o-TIE-ran-us

Eotyrannus was an early relative of the mighty *Tyrannosaurus* from the end of the Age of Dinosaurs. But it was much smaller than *Tyrannosaurus* was. *Eotyrannus* hunted small prey in the swamps, leaving footprints behind in the mud.

Track makers today

Wading birds on a mud bank leave footprints showing where they have been. Dinosaurs like *Eotyrannus* once left their footprints in the mud, too.

Size Comparison

Eotyrannus prowled across the swamp, leaving behind its three-toed footprints. Millions of years later, fossils of these footprints have been found in rocks.

Where Did They Go?

Dinosaurs are extinct, which means that none of them are alive today. Scientists study rocks and fossils to find clues about what happened to dinosaurs.

People have different explanations about what happened. Some people think a huge asteroid that hit Earth caused all sorts of climate changes, which caused the dinosaurs to die. Others think volcanic eruptions caused the climate change and that killed the dinosaurs. No one knows for sure what happened to all of the dinosaurs.

GLOSSARY

armor—protective covering of plates, horns, spikes, or clubs used for fighting

claws—tough, usually curved fingernails or toenails

conifer—trees that produce cones and have needle-like leaves

fossils—the remains of a plant or animal that lived between thousands and millions of years ago

herd—a large group of animals that move, feed, and sleep together

horsetails—simple, non-branching plants related to ferns, with jointed stems and tiny leaves

needles—the long, thin leaves of conifer trees

plates—large, flat, usually tough structures on the body

prey—an animal that is hunted and eaten for food

spikes—sharp, pointed growths

swamp—wet, spongy ground thick with plants

upland—any high ground

To Learn More

More Books to Read

Clark, Neil, and William Lindsay. *1001 Facts About Dinosaurs.* New York: Dorling Kindersley, 2002.

Dixon, Dougal. *Dougal Dixon's Amazing Dinosaurs.* Honesdale, Penn.: Boyds Mills Press, 2007.

Holtz, Thomas R., and Michael Brett-Surman. *Jurassic Park Institute Dinosaur Field Guide.* New York: Random House, 2001.

On the Web

FactHound offers a safe, fun way to find Web sites related to topics in this book. All of the sites on FactHound have been researched by our staff.

1. Visit *www.facthound.com*

2. Type in this special code: 1404847197

3. Click on the FETCH IT button.

Your trusty FactHound will fetch the best Web sites for you!

Index

Look for other books in the Dinosaur Find series:

Bambiraptor and Other Feathered Dinosaurs

Baryonyx and Other Dinosaurs of the Isle of Wight Digs in England

Camarasaurus and Other Dinosaurs of the Garden Park Digs in Colorado

Chungkingosaurus and Other Plated Dinosaurs

Deinocheirus and Other Big, Fierce Dinosaurs

Diceratops and Other Horned Dinosaurs

Pawpawsaurus and Other Armored Dinosaurs

Torosaurus and Other Dinosaurs of the Badlands Digs in Montana

Tsintaosaurus and Other Duck-billed Dinosaurs

Xiaosaurus and Other Dinosaurs of the Dashanpu Digs in China